T0149910

Every Day
A
Holy Day

Exercises, Experiments
and Practices for
Mindful Living

Every Day
A
Holy Day

Exercises, Experiments
and Practices for
Mindful Living

Barbara Haynes

Gateways Books and Tapes
Nevada City, California

Distributed by Gateways Books and Tapes
P.O. Box 370
Nevada City, CA 95959
1-800-869-0658
530-271-2239

www.idhhb.com
www.gatewaysbooksandtapes.com
ISBN Softcover 978-0-89556-278-4

Library of Congress Cataloging-in-Publication Data

Names: Haynes, Barbara, 1950- author.
Title: Every day a holy day / [Barbara Haynes].
Description: Nevada City, CA : Gateways Books and Tapes, 2016.
Identifiers: LCCN 2016018754 | ISBN 9780895562784
Subjects: LCSH: Mindfulness (Psychology)--Problems, exercises, etc. |
Self-actualization (Psychology)--Problems, exercises, etc. |
Awareness--Problems, exercices, etc.
Classification: LCC BF637.M56 H38 2016 | DDC 158.1076--dc23
LC record available at https://lccn.loc.gov/2016018754

Dedicated to
My BelovedTeacher
E. J. Gold

"BEST, MOST COMPREHENSIVE SPIRITUAL EXERCISE BOOK EVER WRITTEN."

— Osho

Introduction

First and foremost, the question is: Who is the author of a book, and is their life an example of what they're writing about? So many spiritual books and teachings are at our fingertips these days, many of which are written by brilliant and charismatic individuals. Yet, how are we to know whether or not someone truly lives according to the "philosophy" they are speaking about? This is of utmost importance. Words may be inspiring and clear and convincing, yet if they are not coming from a person who walks their talk and practices what they preach, the words will definitely not impact us deeply beyond our intellect.

Ms. Haynes has dedicated her entire life to embodying the exercises that she generously offers us in *Everyday a Holy Day*. In this title, she goes right to the core consideration of living a spiritual life. It is that we have a stable sense of the holy and sacred world in which we live. There is so much confusion and aggression around most of us, which makes it challenging to remember that this world is holy. To have an ongoing feeling of the sacred in the midst of being barraged with technology, entertainment, consumer products, and addictions, is not easy.

Potent and reliable medicine is needed to bring our attention back to what our hearts long for. Ms. Haynes' book is such medicine, offering us a palette of gentle yet powerful possibilities. We can easily use our natural instinct to know which ones fit us like a glove. These are exercises that Ms. Haynes has tested throughout the past 30 years. They are not theoretical suggestions, but rather what she has discovered to be transformative. And what she offers can be seamlessly applied in our daily lives.

This book is not about having a peak experience, although these exercises can be a catalyst for this. Ms. Haynes is pointing us to a way to live our lives, which all authentic teachings are about, to be one with our environment and the people with whom we relate. She gives us a lifetime of keys to keep unlocking the doors and deepening our relationship to our heart's desire.

Purna Steinitz
Bozeman, Montana
June 22, 2016

Author's Preface

I first came across the idea of using exercises or experiments to open new perspectives on myself, the environment and my relationships with others when I encountered E.J. Gold's book *Practical Work on Self* in 1984. Mr. Gold offers exercises in his book that allowed me to gain a new understanding of myself.

I worked with each of the twenty-four exercises in *Practical Work on Self* and found the results revealing.

I had a most profound experience while doing the "Popcorn" exercise.

I was driving my car – a stick shift – and attempting to watch the movements of my body doing its job while keeping an eye on traffic. Suddenly "things" changed. Though traffic continued, it felt as if everything had gone into slow motion, I could see around the car in a way that would not normally have been possible – more like a sensing than a seeing. I drove another five or ten minutes in that state before I arrived home. When I left the car I had a definite feeling of having been cared for ever so gently by the car and I gave it a pat on the trunk in thanks. I walked through the house and finally sat down on the sofa where I enjoyed another half hour of heightened perceptions.

One Wednesday afternoon, about a year ago, as I was preparing dinner, I had the thought: how easy it would be to keep the kitchen clean and exercise my attention if I remembered all the things and areas I had touched during meal preparation and made sure to clean them during clean up.

My Wednesday afternoon meal prep inspiration got me to thinking about the various little exercises, experiments and practices I have done over the years and the ones I currently do to strengthen my attention and presence. I decided to gather them together and share them.

At one time or another, I have done all the exercises in this book. Some have become a part of my life while others I pick up and put down as the need arises. They have all come from personal experience personally experienced.

The exercises are not in a particular order. I encourage you to use them in whatever way works best for you. Opening the book and letting synchronicity take a hand in choosing which one you will do that day is a great way to approach the exercises. Keeping a journal can help you work with the experiences you have as you do the different exercises.

I hope you will find this book useful and that it will inspire you to find ways to make every day a holy day.

Barbara Haynes
Grass Valley, Ca.
2016

Kitchen Hands

While cooking a meal, notice what your hands touch. Spice jars, salt shakers, and drawer handles are some of the things that come to mind. When cleaning up after the meal preparation, be sure to clean those places, items, utensils, etc. that you touched while you were cooking. As you wash each of the items used in your daily meal preparation, reconnect with the time during your meal preparation you used the item.

Attitude of Gratitude

As you prepare food, generate an attitude of gratitude toward the food for its willingness to sacrifice itself to feed you, your family and friends.

Guests

As you prepare a meal, picture the people who will be eating the meal. They may be family members, friends, business associates or people you may not as yet know. See them enjoying and benefiting from the meal you are preparing.

Plates

As you serve the plate for each individual at the table, say a blessing prayer for that person.

Silence

No talking in the kitchen. This can begin as a three to five minute exercise. As you repeat it, increase the time, in increments, with which you are comfortable. The goal is to be able to practice silence during the entire time you are cooking. Communication directly related to the preparation of the meal is allowed.

Do Talk

Work with a friend in the kitchen and talk to your heart's content. Notice the difference, if any, between the experience of not talking while working in the kitchen and talking while working in the kitchen.

Stay Put

Once you come to the kitchen to cook a meal, do not leave the kitchen to attend to other business, unless it is an emergency. Do not make phone calls or step out of the kitchen to handle anything other than getting necessary supplies stored outside the kitchen or setting the table.

Do Leave

Let yourself come and go from the kitchen as you prepare a meal. Do you notice any difference in the quality of the experience, in the timing or sense of the space created for the meal?

Special Object

Pick an object that you pass by many times a day. Establish a specific pattern in relation to this object. Walk around the object, touch it, nod to it. Create a subtle ritual which you perform each time you encounter your chosen object.

Something New

As you walk into a familiar room, notice something new. Do this for each familiar room you enter throughout the day.

Notice Me

When you walk into a room, what do you see first? As you do this throughout the day, observe if you have a tendency to notice certain types of things more than others.

Notice Me Two

What is the first color you see when you walk into a room? Do you notice one color more than others?

Room

Which element in a room defines it for you? What would the room be without this element? What makes the music room the music room? If you took the piano out of the music room, would it still be the music room?

Smelly Rooms

What do you smell in the different rooms and places you encounter during the day? Do the smells remind you of other places, times, emotions or events?

Smelly Places

Today, as you travel from place to place, notice the differences in the smells you encounter. If you closed your eyes, would you be able to know where you were? How does it make you feel? Does it bring up any associations or memories?

Lighting

Notice the lighting in each of the different rooms and spaces you find yourself in today. Does the lighting produce a mood?

Same Room

Pick a room in your home that you frequent every day more than once. Observe the changes in lighting in this room under many different conditions. Morning, noon, evening or at different seasons of the year or with electric light. Notice the differences in this room caused by the change of light.

Same Room Again

Choose a room that you are in at the same time everyday. Notice the changes in the room each time, even though you are there at the same time everyday.

Changeling

As you walk into a room, assume that one of the items in the room is not exactly what it was. Which item is it?

Details

When you find yourself waiting, select an object near at hand and notice all the details possible without moving yourself or the object.

More Details

Pick a room in your home in which you spend a lot of time, then pick an object in that room and study it or "spend time with it" for five minutes every day for a week. After spending five minutes a day for a week with the object, what do you know about the object you didn't know before?

Add Detail

Pick an object in a room you enter and leave several times a day. Each time you go into the room glance at the object and add a new detail to what you have already noticed about your chosen object.

Jumping Color

As you enter a room, notice the color that jumps into your attention. Look at the color. See the play of light, the intensity, the various shades. Watch as the change of light in the room alters the color. Does the color illicit memories or emotions?

More Color

When the one color of the room has flagged your attention, notice where else in the room the color is located.

Color of the Day

Each day for a week, pick a color you will notice for that day. Notice where you find this color most – in offices, outdoors, Dr.'s office. How is it used? On walls, in clothing, furniture? How does the observing of the color seem to affect you? How are the different colors of the different days different?

Keys

As you open a locked door, use your keys to remind you that you are passing from one universe to another. Do not assume you know what is on the other side of the door, even if you have been through that door thousands of times.

Washing Dishes

As each item is cleaned, silently repeat (aloud if you are alone or your housemates are understanding): "Thank you for your service."

Flowing Universe

When riding in a car or traveling in or on other transportation (where you can see the scenery passing by), gradually come to feel that the car, train, bus or subway is not moving, but rather the scenery is flowing by you. The vehicle is standing still while the universe flows past.

Sweep the Floor

(Notice I did not say vacuum the floor.) I prefer to use an old fashioned straw broom in the kitchen. A push broom – one you can use in the garage or on the sidewalk or pathway is also a good candidate for use in this exercise. As you sweep, watch how your body coordinates itself to accomplish the task. Watch as if you are watching a dancer. Be aware that all the movements needed to "sweep the floor" are done without you directing the activity.

Mirror

Look in a mirror. Look past the face you see to the environment behind. Get the feeling that the room you see in the mirror is the real room and the room in which you are standing is the reflection.

Mirror Reflection

Study your reflection in a mirror. Get the feeling that the person in the mirror is the real person and you are the reflection.

Making Faces

Stand in front of your bathroom mirror. Any mirror will do, but I like doing this exercise in the bathroom – don't know why. Make all kinds of faces. Do this every day for a week.

Laughing in the Mirror

Relax your face so that it is basically expressionless. Now, laugh in as many different ways as you can manage without ever changing your expression. As you do this, watch your face in the mirror to be sure that you are not "putting on a happy face."

Cleaning

As you dust, wash, shine, polish or vacuum the various things that you clean, be aware of each object's thingness – it is a vase, a table, tile floor, etc – being the best, whatever it is. Be sure to respect the being/thingness as you clean each object.

Long Hall

When you find yourself walking down a long hallway, focus on the end of the hallway while relaxing the focus of your eyes, so that you can see all doorways and side hallway entrances, as well as the ceiling and floor. Get the sense that the doorways and side hallway entrances are openings into other realities, connecting with the reality you are currently in. The hallway is an artery through which beings move from one reality to another.

Sound

Listen to the environment as if you do not know what the sounds are. Be an auditory illiterate. Do not identify any sound. Notice that each sound has a different feeling, tone, color and vibration. Allowing yourself to listen without identifying the sound may, lead to other ways of perceiving.

Listening

Find a place where you will be surrounded by people who speak a language you do not understand. Listen to the people around you as they speak. Hear the rhythm, tone and speed of the language. Relax and let the sound just be. Notice what effect, if any, not being able to understand those around you has on you.

Street Sounds

If you live in a busy city, this will be an exercise that is easily accessed. When you find yourself in the midst of a very busy and loud city environment, listen to the sounds as if they are musical instruments or conversations of unknown beings. Let go of significance related to the sounds. Let yourself listen for the play between the sounds.

Movie Making

As you go about your day, watch for those happenings that would make a great scene in a movie.

Don't Touch

For three to five minutes a day, do not touch your face. After a week or two, expand the length of time you assign to not touching your face by another three to five minutes – more if you can tolerate it. It is possible to continue expanding the time allotted to not touching your face, until you discover that you have taken on the practice / habit of not touching your face.

New Energy

This exercise builds on the "Don't Touch" exercise. As you are able to not touch your face for longer periods of time, notice if there is a change in your energy. Is your energy more calm? Do you have more energy? Do you feel less distracted? Notice what changes begin to occur as you "Don't Touch."

Instrument

At least once a week during your daily music practice, just listen to how the instrument sounds. Do not strive for correctness; simply let the instrument express itself and listen.

Repeat Yourself

I like to fold laundry as I do this exercise. In particular I find washcloths and towels to be the best for this practice. However, any action that is repetitive will work. As you do the repetitive action, get the feeling you will be doing this forever. How does that make you feel?

Speaking

Before you speak, ask yourself why? If it is not actually necessary, refrain from speaking. As you become successful at holding your speech, you may discover some interesting things about your energy.

Say It Again

At some time during each day, pick a phrase you have just spoken and repeat it in exactly the same way and tone you used the first time. This can be a fun meal time activity, especially with kids.

PMS

When you are depressed, sad, or troubled, behave in a way that will not betray your inner state. For women, if you hear, "I didn't even know you were PMS" from your partner or housemates, you have succeeded at this exercise. As in many practices, it is good to notice any changes in yourself as a result of not manifesting your inner state.

Seeing

Look closely at a plant or animal or human. As a child, I would spend hours observing the world that was contained in the ground at my feet. I would lie on my belly gazing into a miniature world awestruck by the intricate beauty. Even though it was hours, it would seem as minutes to me. I felt as if I had gone on a journey, not of this world. So, find a willing plant, animal or human and take a journey of your own.

Thank You

In this day of automation and cars that talk to us, it seems only appropriate if we thank them when they automatically lock the doors or tell us our keys are still in the ignition. And how about the coffee maker that turns itself on and brews you your first cup, so it's ready when you step from the shower? Or that automatic watering system that saves you dragging the hoses all over the yard? For a day or a week or from now on, say thank you to those unseen automatic helpers.

Meal Time

Sit quietly at your table for five minutes before beginning to eat. Take the time to see the people with whom you will share your meal. See the environment in which you will consume the meal. Notice the sounds and smells of your environment. When your plate is served, see the food on your plate. Acknowledge its willingness to be consumed and used by you.

Special Guest

Have a dinner party and invite someone whom you are not fond of. Treat this particular individual like a precious friend. Make their favorite dish or menu, have their favorite flower, music, etc.

Fuzzy Friends

Treat your fuzzy friends, also known as stuffed toys, as though they are alive. Make sure they are seated where they can see the activity in the room and that they have other fuzzy friends with whom they can have fun. Talk to your fuzzy friends. Also listen – you'd be surprised what they will have to say. Some of my best friends are fuzzy.

Silent Spaces

Observe the silence between sounds.

Pauses

Observe the pause between in-breath and out-breath.

Actor

As you prepare for your day – showering, shaving, putting on makeup, dressing – do it as if preparing for a part in a play. Throughout the day, remind yourself that you got into costume and character to act your part.

Phone

When you answer the phone, visualize a long tunnel-like opening happening between you and the party to whom you are speaking an opening that connects two different dimensions or realities.

Mirror Reminder

Each time you look at yourself in a mirror, remember you are an actor in a play.

Sherlock Holmes

Create a story – a history – about who lives in the room you find yourself in, based on the objects in the room - the way the room is decorated, how neat or not, how clean or not, etc. This would be a great game to play with the family, each individual telling a different history/story. If you don't know why this exercise is called Sherlock Holmes, look him up on the internet – you'll be glad you did.

One Object

Take an object and tell the history of the owner.

Miniature

Look at a miniature scene and think of it as a world in another dimension, rather than a small representation of our dimension. Study it closely – until you really do see the world as its own. Miniature railroad scenes or worlds contained in bottles are good possibilities for this exercise.

Walking Through Air

When walking, feel the air moving across your body, even indoors. Don't change the way you move, but get the idea that you are moving through a substance that is flowing around you.

Say "Thank You"

Say *thank you* to someone every day. Not the automatic thank you that we so often express, but a genuine *thank you*. Perhaps for something thoughtful they always do. Or a small kindness in an otherwise difficult day.

Sit Still

When you find yourself waiting – doesn't matter where – don't move for five minutes. Don't touch your face, don't shift position, don't use mobile devices. Just sit still.

Breath

From time to time, throughout the day, notice your breathing. Without any attempt to change it, simply notice – is it quick, shallow, constricted? Also, notice what emotion you may be feeling at the same time. Just let the breath be what it is. Simply observe. Check in with yourself in this way several times throughout the day.

Reaction

"It's not what's happening that is the problem, it's my reaction to it." Use this mantra any time you need to remind yourself that a change in attitude will change your experience.

Contemplate

As you go about your daily activities at the office, home or school, ask yourself the question: "If I was no longer to do what I do, who would I be?"

Coincidence

Watch for all the coincidences during your day. In the morning, you hear that a friend is going to a small town in South Africa. In the afternoon, you are in a waiting room, reading an article about that very town. You and a friend have a conversation about an old movie and then there it is on the movie channel. Keep your attention on the possibilities of coincidence – they are everywhere.

Precognition

You think of someone and they walk into the room or call. I have a light outside my front door, that, during the winter, I never turn off. The other day out of nowhere, I thought about the light bulb burning out. When I returned later that evening, it had burned out. Precognition can be about big things or little things. Notice it throughout your day.

Watch the Movie

For five minutes – or as long as you can tolerate it - watch only the background in a movie. Do not watch the actors.

Watch the Movie Again

For five minutes – or as long as you can tolerate it – watch only the actors. Do not watch the background.

Watch the Movie Three

Turn the sound off on the movie for five minutes or longer – whatever you can tolerate. Notice the difference, if any, in the way you relate to the movie.

Living Food

As you prepare fruits and vegetables for cooking and consumption, notice their aliveness.

Elijah

Prepare a special meal for yourself only or for you and some very special guests. When you set the table, set it for one more than the number of guests. This extra place is for Elijah. You may serve food or not to this extra place. This exercise can be seen as a way to remind ourselves of the presence of spirit at all times.

Eating

When eating, sit with your food, give it all your attention. Do not stand, watch TV or a movie. Sometimes, if you have understanding companions, you may even have a meal where everyone is silent until the consumption of the food is complete.

Hands

Find an activity in which your hands are fairly active - washing dishes, typing, sewing, needle work or gardening. Watch your hands as they go about their business. Allow yourself to really be aware of how they move and how the things they touch feel.

Read to Another

Read aloud to at least one other person, regardless of age. Read what you think they would find interesting, comforting, funny, inspirational or something you would just like to share. If you are alone, then picture the person you want to read to and read to them.

Read Aloud

As you read aloud, hold the person to whom you are reading in your attention with the intention to transmit to them the story. Listen to your voice and how it conveys the story, but do not be dramatic. See the images suggested by the story and send them on to those who are listening.

Do Touch

Next time you are in a fabric or yarn store or bamboo clothing store, touch the different fabrics, yarns and clothing. Notice the difference in each texture. Notice your reaction. Does it bring up memories? Does it change your mood?

Taste It

When you eat, actually taste your food. Try to determine the different spices and/or herbs that were used.

Day's End

At the end of the day, ask yourself the two questions my daughter, Hava, asks her children: How was your day? What was good or special about it?

Passwords

Choose a password for an account you use often that will remind you of a spiritual aim you are currently working with.

Tone

Listen to the tone of someone speaking. It's even better if you can't actually hear the words but only the tone. Determine what the communication is about strictly from tone.

Multi-Task

Disallow yourself from multi-tasking for half an hour. Do not be distracted by anything. Do only one task for that half hour. You may discover that you actually get more done with less stress by doing only one task at a time.

Habit

Choose a small insignificant habit and change some part of it. If you put your right shoe on before your left, then change it to the left shoe before the right. If you carry your keys in one pocket or a specific part of your purse, change that place.

Is It Clean?

When you think you've cleaned a pot, inspect it with your eyes and your hands. Close your eyes when touching the pot. If there are any bumps on the surface, open your eyes and clean that spot. Repeat this look and feel until the pot looks and feels clean.

Be Quiet

As you put away the dishes and pots from the dishwasher or drainer, make as little noise as possible. Move slowly and place each object carefully.

Who's There

Each time you read aloud, notice how the attention of the listeners changes the quality of the reading.

Only Do

When engaged in routine activities such as brushing your teeth, washing dishes or folding laundry, all of which seem to invite or allow all kinds of mind chatter, scenario building, self-arguments, etc., bring your attention back to just doing. Feel the toothbrush in your mouth, watch your hands fold the laundry or wash the dishes. Only do.

Still Small Voice

Answer the still small voice. The one that says, "Make that call now. Listen to the news. Don't go to the movies. Do the laundry now." What I know about the still small voice is that it talks to me about all kinds of things great and small. When I listen and do, I find myself in the flow of things.

Door Mantra

Choose a mantra that you will repeat each time you pass through a doorway. I like to use the phrase "I am here," because it is short and simple. Choose a mantra with which you resonate and which will bring you into the moment.

Don't Complain

For one day, do not allow yourself to complain. If you hear yourself begin to complain, simply cut the comment short. Next time, catch yourself before you get started. Notice how many times you stop yourself from complaining.

Stairs

Count the number of steps you climb as you ascend or descend a staircase.

See It Again

Find a movie you really like. View it every day for a week. Notice something new about the movie each time.

Barefoot

Walk barefoot across your lawn, your carpeted floor, the bathroom tiles or a mud puddle. Feel your feet on the floor or ground. Be aware of the texture of what you are walking on.

Intention

For a week set an intention for each day, like saying a phrase at a certain time or doing a particular action at a specified time.

Transition

Before entering your home at the end of your work day, take a pause to recognize the transition between your work world and your home world.

Brush Your Teeth

Each time you brush your teeth, place your attention on the feeling of the toothbrush in your mouth, the sound of the brushing, the taste of the toothpaste – be there for the time you brush your teeth.

Always Clean

When you come into the kitchen, wash your hands before preparing any food. If you touch something that is not clean, wash your hands again. Be aware of each time you touch something that is not clean. Wash your hands each time.

Pick A Phrase

Pick a phrase from your favorite book. Perhaps your favorite spiritual book or a great kids book. Contemplate the phrase throughout the day.

Late

Don't be late. If you find that you are consistently late, pick one meeting or event that you attend regularly and be on time for that meeting or event.

Hurry

When it is necessary to do things quickly, do them quickly without hurrying. Hurrying is a state of mind and a dramatization of one's upset or stress.

Make Their Day

As you check out at the supermarket or other checkout line, make sure to really interact with the person at the register. Tell them a joke or give them a compliment – really engage them in a way they will remember at the end of their day.

To-Do List

There are all kinds of items on a to-do list. Every day take a break and take your attention off your to-do list and put it on just what you are doing – whatever it is.

Do Unto Others

Find one thing each day that you would appreciate someone doing for you and do it for someone else. Get the car washed, pick up the kids, do the laundry, cook a meal, do the dishes - everyday things.

Anonymous

Do the same as Do Unto Others, only make sure no one knows you've done the deed.

Be Late

If you are a consistently on time person, allow yourself to be five minutes late to an event once a day for a week - if possible. Observe the reactions within yourself. What emotions do you feel? What thoughts do you have?

Season Change

Watch the incremental changes in the atmosphere, vegetation, lighting, smell, temperature, humidity, as each season moves into the next.

Bored Meetings

As you sit in a difficult meeting, or one that is stressful, or perhaps just plain boring, with thoughts of how you wish you could change the situation, turn that wish around and wish to change yourself. Rather than resisting "what is," imagine yourself to be relaxed and accepting of "what is". Get a sense of rightness with the world as it is happening – including your reaction to it. You can't change what is, but you can learn to like it, or at least make good use of it.

Emotion

As you experience an intense emotion from joy to anger, look at your posture, facial expression, body tensions. Listen to the tone of voice and volume of your speech. Are you sweating? Is your heart beating faster? Are you gasping for breath? Notice if any changes occur in you as a result of observing the experience.

Reminder

Wear a special piece of jewelry, clothing or scent. Each time you become aware of the jewelry, each time you feel the clothing, or each time you smell the scent, say a predetermined prayer or mantra. Remember who you are and to what you are connected.

Pick An Action

Pick an action that you do habitually, and each time you see yourself doing the action, say a prayer or mantra. Remember who you are and to what you are connected.

Pick A Posture

Another variation on Reminder. Decide on a posture that you habitually repeat and each time you find yourself in that posture, say your prayer or mantra. Remember who you are and to what you are connected.

Automatic

Notice throughout your day how many things are done by you in an automatic way. Brushing your teeth, making coffee, driving the car, attending a meeting, greeting co-workers – the list could get very long. Make a list of these automatic behaviors.

Make It Yours

Choose one of the automatic behaviors on your list and make it intentional. Rather than just sliding into the behavior, do it intentionally. Notice how doing this makes you feel.

Irritation

Over the period of a month, pay special attention to what irritates or angers you about someone else. Each time you notice yourself upset about that trait, ask yourself "Is that in me?".

Admiration

Over the period of a month, notice the things that you admire about someone else. Ask yourself "Is that in me?".

Touch

Make a ritual of folding your laundry. Fold each similar piece the same way and stack them in an orderly manner. Notice the color and texture of each item you fold.

Honor the Dead

On the anniversary of the death of someone you know, do something they would have done or would have enjoyed doing.

No Timer

If you habitually use a timer for cooking vegetables. Use your attention and focus instead. Notice the color and firmness of the vegetables as they cook. Cook them until they reach a "doneness" you would enjoy at a meal. Even though you may cook a certain vegetable frequently, it is never actually the same vegetable. The timing will be different. That's why using attention and focus rather than a timer will yield more finely cooked vegetables.

My Tone

Listen to your own tone of voice in your conversations today. Does your tone convey something different from the words you are speaking or the body language you are using?

Put It Back

When you take an object from its place to use it, always return to that same place. Put the hammer back in the toolbox, the vacuum back in the closet, the cereal back on the shelf, the butter back in the fridge. Just put it back.

Interruption

If you are interrupted in the middle of an action or project and cannot delay the interruption, treat the interruption as a death point. You will not be able to ask Mr. Death to wait while you finish your email, so this is good practice for leaving one universe and moving on to the next.

Alphabetical Index of Exercises

Index of Illustrations

About the Author

Barbara Haynes was born in 1950 to a tenant farming family on the plains of west Texas. Her mother was a devout Christian and instilled in Barbara a sense of spiritual values and a belief in an existence beyond what we can see. She spent her early adult years searching for a spiritual "home".

In the spring of 1984 she received an invitation to attend, what was for her a pivotal, invocational dinner at which the work of E.J. Gold was presented and studied. She found the works of E.J. Gold and his presentation of the ideas to be very practical and useful in everyday application.

After working with Mr. Gold and some members of his community at a jewelry show in Los Angeles in 1985 Barbara made the decision to move to California to live and work with the community working with Mr. Gold.

In November, 1986, Barbara moved to Grass Valley, California and has been working closely with Mr. Gold for the last thirty years.

Dear Reader,

If you enjoyed this book and found it useful, we encourage you to explore the books below.

Practical Work on Self	E.J. Gold
Just Because Club	Claude Needham, PhD
Spiritual Gaming	E.J. Gold
The Great Adventure	E.J. Gold

For an indepth exploration of our spiritual nature and how to Wake Up, see the offerings at Gateways Books and Tapes - gatewaysbooksandtapes.com. If you are interested in the work of E.J. Gold and the community of IDHHB, visit http://idhhb.com/ or at Prosperity Path Forum on Facebook
https://www.facebook.com/search/top/?q=prosperity%20path.

We can also be reached at 1-800-869-0658 or 530-271-2239 or by mail:

IDHHB, Inc.
P.O. Box 370
Nevada City, Ca. 95959

Sincerely,
The Editors
Gateways Books and Tapes